# 60
# CONVERSATIONS
*for* TOMORROW

# 60 CONVERSATIONS
# for TOMORROW

by

**Dennis J. Reader**

www.sempervirensbooks.com

Published 2023 by Sempervirens Books

Cover design and graphics by GDM

ISBN (paperback) 979-8-9855825-0-5
ISBN (hardback) 979-8-9855825-1-2

FOR FURTHER INFORMATION OR OTHER BOOKS BY THE AUTHOR GO TO:
www.sempervirensbooks.com

*This little book is an eternal big hello
to my children and grandchildren*

# ---*Contents*---

# PART ONE

## 20 Conversations

*We will speak tomorrow's talk today.*

# Big Mortality Talk with Little You

5 billion x 365 the earth has spun
we hear, or thereabout,
with 5 billion x 365 turns more to come.
What a faithful dreidel, but now
I know you know for sure
it will absolutely stop.

Already at merely 365 x 10 you can
dream, take the impossible trip back
to forgotten sunrises over a sulfur sea
illuminating blank continents of rock,
every day once waking its ancient way
into what we now call "Good morning!"

You try to picture each separate time a sunset
has had to unwind and scatter pretty colors
into the absorbent night, another brave show
before another dark sleep, one more promise
of endless encores you know it will not keep.

Unhappy you study me, you do, stroke
(sort of) my hand with a grander touch
than this grandfather can, and you
try hard to speak those hard words
that always hurt a loving heart.

Let us sit together often, just like this,
right until a day I disappear—agreed?
Together we will watch at breakfast
dewy nets of glitter tangle on our lawn,
at dinner our sky kissed lipstick pink.
We will speak tomorrow's talk today.
Remember later I never dared complain
going away, since this chromatic globe,
especially dear vivid you, must follow
pale me to fade the same.

# Valediction Rehearsal

He tries hard not to laugh
when each&every morning
she runs on frantic little feet
and bending he accepts
an absurdly urgent squeeze,
its fiery need, the grand farewell,
a most solemn and comic drama.

In his car, in traffic, in trouble
according to his ruthless watch
he leaves behind that charming frown,
that taste of oatmeal when she demands
a "bwig fat kwiss" then quickly adds
her oh-so-clever "please."

He soon forgets the way the rising moon
pokes white fingers past curtain corners
to touch exactly just her black bed.
Was it today he turned back
to wave? Or maybe yesterday?
He never remembers either, is it
pears she likes or peaches?
Did he ever notice, even once before,
how when his daughter says goodbye
she guesses other absences
they have to practice for?

## Some Rhymes for a Child
## Fatherless in the Womb

Hello little nameless thing,
little boy or girl (to be), listen to me
from inside your wet maternal swim,
while I search for shade in a distant desert.

Listen, little daughter or son, for I knew the one
who will never speak, the dad in the photograph,
the question waiting in your unborn thoughts,
the absent memory, the true guy, your missing key.

Oh yes, I even saw him die, without much asking why
because dying happens here, every now and then,
where soldiers carry guns and where we discover duty
and get paid for being very scared and kind of brave.

Down an empty and ugly road we drove
toward a point on a map, when *voilà* a magic noise
undressed his clothes into three separate piles,
folded flat there in the dust, but enough of that.

I had no chance to squeeze his shoulders
like he did mine once, that wretched time
when I was sick, or drunk to tell the truth, and he
helped chase away the blood of a red-red-red day.

So I think a lot about what should have been,
when you two took first steps together off
to wherever, some history of smiles and scowls,
dancing the long dance called Father & Child.

I have it wrong? Maybe better is, you need
a real face to take his place instead,
a living voice that can whisper late at night,
"Love you. No, no, I won't turn out the light."

*(Some Rhymes for a Child Fatherless)*

I know for sure he wishes you any luck
and any daddy that come along your way.
And let me say to ease those future doubts,
never worry you left him behind alone.
More each day he becomes the father to me.

# How I hate a circle

How I hate a circle
for all its lazy symmetry,
its stubborn certitude.
Circle is circle
only
whether great or small,
plodding in a path around a post.
See centripetal
beside me again&again
the falling father
and rising son?

Find for me, somewhere,
a broken line pointing
off,
a finger of defiance
or of mutant chance:
such a glory,
such a heathen's joyous shout,
such a soaring from the course,
free
to fly and skid and smash.
No one holds the axis nor
turns its dagger point nor
sweeps the brutal arc.

# You & Me

Never will they say about me
or you
that school teachers shook with joy
(and fright) to find there before them
Galileo or Newton in a child's body.

Whatever they might praise
for us
if they praise at all,
it can never equal
"We first found the Mozart boy!"

For us
obedient we await the dusk,
to follow, blank moons rising easterly
and not the sun,
our only feat: we too rose, we too set.

Let solace enough
for us
be that light lacks heat, a sun its beacon
or glory, without our skin to feel, our eyes to see,
and loyal moons to mirror triumph through the night.

# 14 February: Pathology Report

I asked you to grow
in my scarlet garden.
Agreed, we planted the seed
I think with a kiss
then buried it all away.

Winter went, winter came again,
before I noticed in the cold
the fever that would not leave.
A parasite sucks my strength I feared,
some intruder wants to wear my skin.

You took a closer look,
a shovel in your hands,
and smiled digging down so deep
to turn up such good news:
"My root has cracked your rock."

# Vorläufige Liebe

"Hin ist immerhin hin"
hast du mir geweint
(ja Tränentreu)
deinen Mund aber voll
von Faselei:
3mal *hin*.
Selbst das Klischee hinkt.

Einst
schöne Liesli, warst du
Künstlerin der Sprache
für mich, schufst Farben
und Hitze um Mitternacht
mit Worten bloß.

Verzeih, wenn mein Erstaunen
wie ein Schrei klingt.
Leider
keiner hat mich je
gelehrt, dass Kunst verfallen
kann.

Gestern war ich einzigartig
in der Welt,
ein Museumstück insgeheim.
Heute bin ich wieder Karl,
alltäglicher Name
einsilbig
und gemein.

# Temporary Love

"An end is an end's end"
you sobbed to me
(with such suitable tears)
your mouth however
packed full with drivel:
3 x *end*.
Even the cliche falls flat.

Once
lovely Liesli, you were
an artist of speech
for me, created colors
and heat at midnight
with words alone.

Pardon, if my surprise
sounds more a scream.
Sadly
nobody ever taught me
that Art can decay
away.

Yesterday I was unique
in the world,
a secret museum piece.
Today I am Karl again,
ordinary name
single syllable
and plain.

# The Almost Unprepared Poet

My heart jumps. A stranger, you
suddenly knock outside on the door.
Since this place is called my poem,
and since you seem a seeker, quite alone,
I must invite you in for food and succor.

Been looking long? And far, yes?
I duly confess a sweaty surprise
to find us together like this: you
so tired, hunger in your face, me
with empty white spread on the plate.

My inhospitality is such a sin.
I hope to pay sharp punishment
for your weariness and your want,
for your precious time,
for my squandered space.

They say "Every paper kills a tree."
For its wasteful death
and your hurtful life,
I'm sorry, friend,
sorry.

Or not. Not so sorry if
this is just my own old mirror talk
full only of more old self reflections.
I should have remembered before how
nobody else eats poems anymore.

# Simple Lies for a Simple Poem for a Simple Tragedy

*1.* Indians never smile.
*2.* Morticians don't cry.
*3.* Tall is better than short.
*4.* Angels can't die.

I couldn't swear exactly
why the first three lie,
but I do love an Angela
and this Angela did die.

# On the Honeymoon of a (N)e(u)rotic Groom

Dark it is.
Streetlights, hoping to invade our room,
Halo the pillow under your magic hair.
Alone we are. Other faces, voices,
All public performances—gone.

Our moment we have: skin with skin,
Love with love. The world pointed us
Here, and now the whole world waits.

Freed from beneath its cloth shell
Escapes your waiting heat
Which ignites at once my own.
I fasten to the thick blushing button
Over your heart, undo and do and undo
It again. And then, when

In the middle of too much happiness
(Please damn my soul
Or cure my sick chemistry)
I deconstruct you dear Stephanie,
Hearing a pump deep below
Squeeze your precious blood.

I peel apart the tight tiny bud, called
*Flora umbilicus*, that plugs the tunneled way
To your secret gastro-archipelago, colored
Tahitian green, looped with purple&pink lagoons,
Surrounded by a virgin continent of colon.

My weepy tears? Ignore them.
Just let this autopsy continue,
Caressing future ovarian cysts,
Fondling aroused lymph nodes,
Until in our rising symphony I hear
Undertones: the clank-clank-clank
Of dry bones-bones-bones.

# Western Wind No. 2

*(For the unknown singer, circa 1500)*

First
the sighing, as if out of sight
somewhere over on the west field's other side,
acres and acres away, a young god lay moaning
for his absent springtime love.

Next
the moist breath
to stroke budded trees, caress
new grass, embrace buildings,
seek warmth to join its warmth.

Then
with sudden pant comes on the window
a windslap and a raintap,
and I stretch back, my own young god, with
my own small rain and my love in my arms again.

# The Heartbreak of Hemispheres

Say it plain,
Pain and all:
I am autumn old.
You are maiden young,
Those reluctant buds
That cap your breasts afraid to flower.
I scare off songbirds that promise you
Twelve full months of spring.

Green is your favorite color, brighter
The better, while I wear heavy golds.
Feeling a chill in my breath
And meaning, you shiver,
Fretting over changed complexion.
Now even when yearning toward me
You flee, seeking perfect sun.

Beware, fine princess.
Spring grasses are the softest
But bear no seeds.
Yet I might run with you
Despite my anchored antipode.
My love, tell me how we tip the globe.

# My Middle-Aged Mrs. A

Darling, let us admit impediment.
Call it time, dust on the lens, gravity on
Flesh, yellowed paper, five children, wore tires,
Less hair, bad budgets, old quarrels, October frost,
Fatigue—call it whatever we will, but it's clear
We're not what we were.

Now let us grope
Backward, where backward is ahead,
Roll a continent of virgin dirt over rust,
Rename mountains, plant forests, explore slowly
What we pioneered so fast.
And if we see that other ocean in the distance,
And the end of land, let us feel the world
Watching again, as once again
We try out fine new dreams
To fail.

# Remembering the Coldest War
### *(1950-1953)*

When we were both twenty the world
Turned cold, and he got wrapped up
Like a gift from Korea and mailed home.

That year a wind cut through our houses
And his mother brought boxes of clothes,
All familiar, all a perfect match for size.

Inside his blue suit with his blue shirt
My skin went blue, my teeth chattered,
I *froze*, and sent every heavy box back.

Since that season I traveled decades over
Dead men's bridges, worked and slept in
Dead men's buildings, read centuries of

Dead men's words. I married a
Dead man's daughter. Nathan, why
Did I waste your precious warmth?

# Theology for Kids

Whilom it was writ
In a table of content-
Ments that falling stars
Drop from heaven, really.

And what was heaven without
A god, a good big one (or
Better) a big good One?

But on a sunny suspicious midnight
Down in deep-forested Cranium Basin
Wizard woman bubbled her kettle, cackled
About "crooked straight lines, too too unsolid
Flesh, dead stars," and—in short—raised long
Questions as irreverent, as heretical, as very
Dumb as a hot cross pun:
> *(1) a goosed mother or a smothered goose?*
> *(2) a catty diddle or a fidgety kitty?*
> *(3) a doggone sport or a runaway loon?*
> *(4) a cow high on pure moon?*

Stones were thrown
'Til the King decreed a Happy Forever
After, and no one read such Dumb again
Except you and a few behind closed doors
In the privacy of your own poem.

# Eulogy for an IQ 72

He was, we said,
A silly goose that winged back north
Too soon, to hunker down in Canadian snow
And praise the cold.

More boy than man
He ate his neighbor's pears
Before they even turned gold, thought
Sunsets the same things as dawns.

He would grab us
In a wild hug, just as if
We had done the same to him, once before,
Or he mistook us for the brother or sister he never had.

He hardly learned
Much, learned least that he did not learn,
And acted like curiosity was enough an answer by itself
Or being alive was all to know of life.

So we paid plenty
For this pauper's coffin, stood in a dutiful circle,
Heads down, and bid a long *adieu*
To a Spoon River fool.

# My Favorite Grandma

To explain the new whiskers
On a husband dead two days, the doctor said
"It happens."
Without wonderment she shaved resurrection
All away, poured it down the sink.
Years after, on Sundays, she still catechized
Wide-eyed grandkids: old lips telling plainly
The total we needed to know
Of hair, of nails, of immortality.

Of course there came the day
When instead of talking
She made her point another way,
And although we were hardly children
Anymore we remembered to remember
Her story even louder than before.

# A Miracle at Silver Creek

December rain, uninvited,
Came anyway and beat out
A rousing song
That shook the town awake.

Lazy Silver Creek, now excited,
While dancing to this catchy tune
Changed a bend in a step so wild
Tombstones drowned beneath its feet.

Townsfolk crept down
When the silt cleared
To gawk and wail
At Silver Creek's new boulders.

Oh how they prayed
For God please to part these waters,
To move six feet of cold cold creek
From their tired old fathers.

But Silver Creek stayed,
Just laughed, kept polishing marble
Like it wished to wash silence away
From all those dirty faces.

As for me, when soon I up and die,
Let me be stroked by such a
Resurrection of motion in such a
Paradise of silver devotion.

# Compass Directions: Getting Found

I was lost once.
Somewhere out in Iowa, on a ribbon of country road,
in summer rain, and thunder, lost among cornfields,
lost and lost: Sweetsville, pop. 770.

"Miz Parker, she'll let a room."

1946 it was, with a soldier daddy under the Bataan mud
they said, except
no one could ever find the spot
and I knew only that he was lost too
with rain falling on him like this falling rain from Iowa clouds.
18 I was, a bad age to be lost with America so happy:
one misfit boy not invited to the grand victory party.

"Ain't them California plates, son?"

Crossing a continent, yessir. Going east after a job.
Going maybe just to be in motion.
Going maybe just to have a place to arrive at.
Coaxing a '37 Chevy, a leaky convertible, the top cracked
from sitting in the garage while we waited for the real driver.

"Out there, that's the Parker place."

At the edge of town, rising three stories above the plains,
a lone white house collecting the last afternoon light,
clean in the rain.
Inside the white house a white-haired lank old lady, sharp yet
soft, musing aloud.
>Those bedrooms were really for harvest time.
>An exception would be $2 and a lost boy with wet hair.

*(Compass Directions)*

Third-floor room. Nothing to do but sprawl on the spool bed,
surrounded by other living antiques, watching rain twist lines
on glass: don't bother to turn on any lamp.

Dark in the bedroom, at last. The thumping on the roof gone.
From the upper windows of this white Iowa mountain now
opened great vistas of lightning over black prairie.
>Flares,
>tracers,
>shell-bursts,
>fire in the sky,
>burning lashes against the back of night.
>Mutterings, distant howitzers, grenades,
>a blown ammunition dump.

And underneath, sweeping, lay a vast spread of flatness,
awesome in emptiness with only ranks of cornstocks to stand up,
all in perfect rows, marching from over behind the horizon.
Lost, 18, shadow flickers on the wall.
The heat, the sweat,
half-naked atop the bed,
laboring for anything named sleep.
I must be cautious, turning to hide the beat of my heart.

Other eyes are in the room.

There.
Up on the wall,
among flashing shadows,
a portrait in a heavy gilded frame.
A buried Parker patriarch, bearded, smileless, wearing formal
black, watching me.

Impossible to avoid those eyes.
They smoldered, surely, up through the soil of a nearby family
plot, a begrudged, fenced, fertile square circled by pressing corn.
What had they seen, back before the portrait was?

33

*(Compass Directions)*

Space. Grass. The passing travels of wind.
When he built the sod house, did he see the white mountain?

That counter stare spoke some silent news from darkness.
Greetings, from fathers everywhere.
Across the land, from strange house to strange house,
portrait joined to portrait joined to portrait.
Despite the dark, a necessary weave it makes:
one forgotten face and the pattern breaks.

# Dr. Bell

He lived the last months where he had all the years,
in the old grey house. Old himself, grey himself.
And I stopped by to savor his wine and his talk
since both contained the delicious honesty of decay.
As a young man is free, with a whole life ahead,
so Dr. Bell was free, with no life left.

First on a warm spring noon lacquered yellow, I
came up through drooping waves of honeysuckle
shimmer, fat bees stuck in stupor to the flowers.
A courtesy to an ending in the season of starts
I named it pity, for the family doctor without family
of his own, except his wife away inside the cemetery.

I wielded my questions, my attention, my good will,
and by hot midsummer we were close, Dr. Bell
shuffling across hollow rooms murmuring the chronicles
of Fulton County, an elegant soul erect still against
the gravity of starvation, a coolness in the heat, and
a calmness that would only be matched, or usurped,
by the appearance of his famous adversary.

He was weary of that subject, he said,
tired to the spine of seeing "Help me,
help me," behind every eye he met.

Over chilled watermelon I asked: "Parkington Hurd?"

> *Yes*. Stroke. Glory was the quick answer,
> straight furrows for his forty-acre mind.
> Seven children: they got seven words each.
> Never dared to doubt. Why go scare away
> paradise as sweet as these melons here?

*(Dr. Bell)*

Sunflowers grew taller than men. We walked,
often all the way to his wide shade maple,
sitting and looking one more last time
into slow familiar Tabletop River.

"Johnny Malley?"

> *Yes.* Hunting accident. A shotgun,
> his own uncle pulling the trigger.
> Five full hours of life, three awake.
> He hollered those three hours
> even after his real voice wore out.

Once, Dr. Bell said, he himself had begged:
both for their bodies and his own,
through twilights until lonely dawns,
begging yet never any alms. Humiliation converted him.

"DeMarco, the druggist's son?"

> *Yes.* Kidneys. Age twenty-seven, handsome,
> wordless for forever and a day. I never saw
> a more perfect hate. His stare snubbed death
> right when it came up alongside to say hello.

"Miss Danner?"

> *Yes.* She had what I have now.
> A timid old maid, but how she
> panted to hug death closer, faster.
> Her best lover ever. At the end
> she weighed less than her age.

"Marie. Do you remember Marie?"

*(Dr. Bell)*

Clocks talked.

We went out upon the veranda, and since it was autumn,
we thought to continue on to see the maple's leaves.
Dr. Bell rested, halfway. We turned back.

With a display of secrecy, playing a sudden child,
he hurried me inside to his work desk, drew out
a brittle typescript of his own epitaph:
MORIOR ERGO SUM.
It puts the horse before the Cartesian, he laughed,
gripping me so hard I remembered that his hands
were the first to have ever touched me.

On a Tuesday before Christmas he never answered my
knock at the old grey house,
and never would, having departed
on Monday with the first heavy snow.
Twice now it had happened to me.
I learned the lesson again, how absence
is admission of having loved
and recognition of having been.

# PART TWO

## 20 Life Cycle Songs for My Grandchildren

Let us name you all,
girl and boy,
     IZZY
for today
plus a tomorrow.

# Izzy Infinitum
*(Izzy before the Izzy)*

### i

this timeless time the easiest time:
the safest: the deepest sea of sleep:
Izzy always was, will always be:
catch him here&there, in anything
and anywhere: name her whatever,
this&that: write him out as math:
call her aloud as chemistry: never
will he hear or cipher or care:
Izzy is no less than the beginning and before:
Izzy is no more than the ending and thereafter:

### ii

conduct a symphony of chaos, unfinished:
follow its mad dance of happenstance
right to the edge of absurdity: where Izzy
falls, down into a blind and binding nexus:
in the body of a man: in the body of a woman:
proving that impossible happens just enough
to always be a lie: a wait of forever until now:
wait again in the forever from now until then:

### iii

oh: if a universe had the slightest good sense
or paid the least attention it would understand
to slow a bit and smile: better than that: it should
mark this Izzy moment with a tip of its starry hat:

# Izzy in the Lottery
*(Izzy is)*

passion spasm: in an underworld
where anarchy thrives:
where millions swim
for one to win: it happens:
the astronomical dice: the earthly sum:
a bull's-eye with its prize presented
unnoticed in the dark:
this *Izziness*!
an Izzy thing in familiar form
at last: at last: at last: at last:

nor will we modestly deny:
how our precocious Izzy boy
to crown his triumph
discovers the very best way to die:

# Izzy x Izzy x Izzy
*(Izzy learns how to multiply)*

i

what a whirl of dizzy Izzy
when more of him joins in:
again&
again&
again:
happy after their lengthy trip
this family who have never met
yet are full of hugs and kisses:
"Hello! Hello! By me! By me!
Isn't it wonderful being an Izzy?"

ii

one day: out of the blue: newer than new
and stranger than strange: Izzy feels:
feels:
softer-harder-looser-tighter-cooler-hotter:
whether peace or pain it equals the same
delicious stuff to him:
his lidded sight sees only this appetite:

# Introducing Izzy

i

on a wall a machine
called a clock: tick-tock:
on a scheme
called a day and an hour:
draw a line exactly at this spot:

roll the drums
for the greatest of debuts:
a forcing forth
into lights bright on stage:
ahhh's and applause
as our actor appears: kicking a fancy jig:
singing with his own loud Izzy mouth
that favorite hit:
"I'll Never Never Go Away!"
unless it was (they sound alike)
"I'm Absolutely Here to Stay!"

ii

the audience circles to watch him sleep
after his big drama and trauma fatigue:
folding the blanket back, they wonder
who they recognize
in the shape of this new face
while they hide
their grander question:
"With Izzy what have we wrought
on behalf of our human tribe?"

# Izzy's Imperium

Izzy commands: all obey:
Izzy rules his own imperial way:

eat: sleep: wake: wash: 8 pounds
shift the orbit of the social globe:
new mass/new path/new speed:
need: need: need: need:

so: we vassals do as do
servants of any perfect prince:
love/admire/serve:
and plot the coming coup:

# Silly Izzzzzzzy

*yeeeoowww*:
this was really great:
really it was really really great
like a giant stack of sugar zizzles
always waiting on his dinner plate
for him to try-try-try
to eat-eat-eat 'em all
or: what the heck: fling a few at the wall
or zizzle rhyme as much as he might choose
and vomit 'em up right on Opa's shoes:

he really really could do
whatever Izzy wanted to:
fly a kite in a zoo at night
catch a fish in a chafing dish
have a talk with a piece of chalk
grow his toes upon his nose
eat lots more fresh dinosaur
run far away to yesterday:

ooh: it was sooo fine
at absolutely any time
just to rush off and play
in the fun house of Izzy's mind:

# Izzy in the Mirror of His Mind
*(Izzy meets Izzy)*


Izzy sees himself seeing himself
in his mother's mirror
one very surprising day: quite young
quite old enough finally to figure out
the Greatest Show on Earth:


the face inside
the face outside
joining: proving the fact
of an IZZY: an Izzy who shows
in pantomime: "All this is all mine":


here I am there I am
what I am: Izzy thinking:
Izzy thinking of Izzy thinking:
repeating the honored bookish wisdom
of knowing how to know *cogito ergo cogito*:

# Izzy Meets His Worst Best Friend

i

Izzy while happily at play
saw a kid's finger fall off
when a big red piece of it got
caught between metal and pain:

ii

Izzy while in a cute little suit
(but without a tie)
saw a father's father flat
forever on his back:

iii

Izzy while deep in bed and dark
pinched Izzy to make him hurt:
"You: and you you *Izzy*:
would do all that to *me*?"

# Izzy Eats an Apple

### i

Izzy ate a pretty apple:
by the way he stole it first
more or less or more than less:
he knew Mrs. Franks had said
"It's the best one on my tree":

### ii

and not a timid biblical bite
he gobbled the whole thing down:
an apple red and ready:
bright and ripe:
quite willing
to be swallowed:

### iii

he could hardly conceive
how any apple could ever taste
sweeter than an apple ever should:
only because he was clever
did he discover:
forbidden *is* the fruit:

### iv

later: poor Izzy: must reconsider
his tiny and tasty sin: when
Mrs. Franks starts stealing back
her delicious smiles to him:

# Izzy Saves His Species

Izzy grinds his teeth: wakes at night:
sweats his bed: spouts more hair
and grows a deeper growl:

he sniffs for scent: prowls the fields:
breaks branches: curls his fists
and runs fast just to feel the strain:

he devours dreams
of otherness:
other skin against his
other breath inside his
other blood into his:

his witless body knows nothing of nations
with their pyramiding hordes: it only sees
a killer tiger hiding by the pond and
the baby starving at the cave today
or freezing in tomorrow's snow:

in Izzy ancient voices shout an answer
to impending doom: breed: breed: breed:
panic is passion's secret fuel:

# Izzy Learns to Count Up to Loneliness

i

it came a day in Izzy's days
when he knew numbers well enough
to count the world: a census task
as vast as foam flecks on the sea:

ii

he found the names of all the nations:
checked them off a map to fix their size
and presence: calculated the chance
that a face would smile just for him:

iii

he read about how human hearts
beat in concert by the billions:
listened to tally their mighty sound:
used the math of his own small drum:

iv

he added up: he waited:
but *in toto* the sum
of Izzy
still equaled: scarcely: 1:

# Izzy Practices Love

i

first love is forever goes the sentiment and the wish:
that tender part of a virgin heart freshly won
must carry on and not be lost
in harder later years and other loves to come:

ii

Izzy alone at a lonely May moment
of November clouds and peekaboo sun
takes a path used before to get away from where
Izzy is now and probably is tomorrow:
down past the houses
behind the hill
into the woods:

iii

at a tree among the trees waits his leafy Izzy cave:
an ancient willow of hidden rooms beside five pools
too shallow and too secret to earn a printed name:
Izzy greets them name or not
knowing here how to talk like sweethearts do
who sometimes never use words at all
but get by with only touch:

iv

Izzy under his tree holds hands
with a fistful of willow leaves:
head against its trunk his lips
on sympathetic skin rehearse:
"I want us always to be an us
and never a you-and-me":

# Seeking Mrs. Izzy

i

Maisy was first:
a sweet spring wind
she bent her skin to the backs of leaves
and rolled alive across April afternoons
touching
touching: but like any wind
when the touching stopped was not:

ii

Dee Dee was second:
a soulful midnight rain
her heartfelt voice close by his ear
pattered perfectly its rising melancholy song:
loud tears and applause collecting
from roof to roof
until only Izzy bringing the closing curtain down
could halt indulgent clapping in the puddled street:

iii

Clara was third:
an early November snow
that comes to mark a season of no nonsense
she covered faded colors with white so right
as snow and pure enough for an abstraction
or her name: calm and quiet as contentment:
logical as crystals and as cold:

*(Seeking Mrs. Izzy)*

iv

Julianne is last:
Julianne is light
waking Izzy to dawn at unexpected hours
both day and night: she shines somehow
without a heat that burns
or bothers to be celestial:
she smiles at him: calls her light a mirror:
the reflection that Izzy sees
when he looks at Julianne:

v

alight he smiles back:

# Mrs. Izzy on the Science of Marriage

The sky lies, my Izzy dear.
We know that's so
even though you and I look up at nights
to find our favorite friend Athena 6, to greet that merry star
while we exchange a customary little kiss.
Poor Athena 6. Her twinkle and her benediction for us
7.7 billion years old and eons cold
are merely the memory of a rearview window wave
before she flew away to die.

And you there across the room, Izzy my love.
You sitting. You standing. You speaking, sending
me those starry blessings of your own.
My Izzy likewise is a shadow, cast by his instant past,
is he not?
Where and when, husband dear,
do we make our quantum magic?
When will we two use the same clock,
reach the same spot,
where I catch up with you
or you with me?

Izzy, we'll discover inside ourselves a method
to dissolve space, to eliminate these lives
of visual histories that hide us from each other.
From all things imagined by time and substance,
we'll take all of time and substance that there is.

I mean to say, my husband,
the true part and the best
about our Athena 6
has always been that little kiss.

# Izzy in the Sun

the sun was warm: the sky was cloudless blue:
Izzy was strong:
as tall, as free, as Izzy would ever grow to be:

he built a bridge: he ruled a town:
he sang a symphony:
he dug an honest ditch for honest money
and unashamed became half rich and saved
to buy his wisdom (plus a few foolish toys):

Izzy worked hard: liked the glare, the heat:
slept with peace and power through the night:
awoke always to another noon of energy:

# Izzy's Izzy

who could have ever thought
that any anything could be better
than what already always was?

yet was and is:
and such an easy trick
producing such a prize:
this gift of duplication
this impossible creation
who will hold your hand
along the passage of your days:

happy with his special magic
he tries for two or three:
finding then a true delight
when Izzy's Izzy was a she:

# Busy Izzy

to awake is to begin:
to begin is a duty
much like waking:

the body must be moved:
seven serious steps into a bathroom
where ritual rescues necessity
and makes it sane
or less dangerous: ablutions in a basin:
devotion to the inside corner of each eye:
more soldier steps
to bureau drawers and closet hangers:
a fulcrum of tangled wires and color shades
to balance there philosophy/rage:

the body must be fed
and what a hero's heart it takes
to contemplate the authority of food:
who can say
obedience to appetite is different
by much
from obedience to disease
except for tasty sugar and the salt:

so stand at attention Izzy:
comb your hair:
march out the door:
and don't forget to love, and
to aim the world straight, and
remember to worry about it being late:
keep on keeping on
until you sleep again:

# Izzy in the Paradox Box

### i

nature mistrusts the fixed form: Izzy's
40 trillion pieces get a little tired:
come a little loose: want to fly away:

### ii

he holds together for a while:
a decade or a day or
whatever he can to help those
who want their Izzy: please:
to just stay:

### iii

he tries to tell them
(and himself)
the logic of each and every game:
to make a start you need an end:

### iv

but no truth troubles more
than truth in contradiction:

## Izzy Writes His Testament

let me: warn you:
it's not eternity
but the turn:

it's not theology
we should study
but touch:

it's not a heaven
that we need
but home:

it's not in faith
we must believe
but us:

for the turn
the touch
the home
the trust
I thank you dear ones:
and bequeath to each
my holy praise:

# yzzI

### i

Izzy sees himself feels himself
walking out the door: down a backward path
taken (remember?) once before:
and leaves behind the sign that reads
Once Upon a Time:

### ii

he floats: he flows:
along a courseless course
without a start or finish
without a clock or calendar
without an up or down
without a yes or no
without even a without:

### iii

then: when enough such emptiness
wheels and wheels inside itself
to equal: *surprise*: another
Once Upon a Time:
he will meet there: almost greet there:
someone's poem about someone's
Izzy:

# PART THREE

## 20 Sillified Tunes for My Grandchildren

But why be silly?
Because
why not
when in every human life a sadness
might be seduced by a careless smile.

# MATCH THESE FAMILIAR EPIGRAMS
# WITH THEIR SILLY *HOMILY GRITS* PARTNER

"Neither a borrower nor a lender be"

"Absence makes the heart grow fonder"

"Curiosity killed the cat"

"Two heads are better than one"

"All's well that ends well"

"You can lead a horse to water, but
you can't make it drink"

"The early bird catches the worm"

"The last straw that broke the camel's back"

"Blood is thicker than water"

"There's more than one way to skin a cat"

"Never put off until tomorrow what may
be done today"

"Better late than never"

"Beggars can't be choosers"

"Beauty is in the eye of the
beholder"

"Haste makes waste"

"Necessity is the mother of
invention"

"Waste not, want not"

"Let sleeping dogs lie"

"Every cat has nine lives"

"A bird in hand is worth
two in the bush"

"Practice makes perfect"

"To know the value of
money, try to borrow some"

# two4one tip
*(Homily Grits #1)*

When you feel plenty hungry
and you need to choose
between a bird close at hand
or two hiding in the bush,
it can often help you decide
if you buy a jug of herbicide.

# The Horse Whisperer
*(Homily Grits #2)*

The best trick
to get your horse to drink
after leading it to water
(an old Texas cowhand once advised me)
is just pick up a bigger stick
and whisper the French word *boucherie.*

# Why the Pirate Wears an Eye Patch
*(Homily Grits #3)*

My sweetie pie understands,
as do I, about beauty
and its beholder.
Nowadays I get nervous
whenever I hold her
because she has another friend
who will hurt my heart
(plus more than that)
if Sweetie wants her beauty back.

## Use Caution: Words Out of Order
### *(Homily Grits #4)*

Until done
tomorrow
put off today
what may be
never.

# An Apple a Day
*(Homily Grits #5)*

Dear good Miss Frafels, while waiting for love,
Practiced long and hard by kissing some apples.
When the right man arrived she stood on tiptoes
And planted a big fat one straight on his nose.
All of which shows, said her smiling new beau,
Practice makes perfect means perfect at practice.

# Always Read the Label, Kitty
*(Homily Grits #6)*

Frankly, we considered ourselves
plain clever, inventing a pet food
made from bark and recycled leather.
Everyone agreed, brilliant indeed,
with an environmental cachet.

But bad news.
Half the cats refused to taste it
while the other half ate it, and died.
Besides the lawsuit, which cost plenty,
we spent *mucho* money on a big study.

Pathologists, chemists, were all deeply serious
about finding the poison in our perfect product.
The dumb nerds only concluded: "very curious."

# True Love Please
*(Homily Grits #7)*

Yes, I do believe a dog
is man's best friend.
Every morning Muggs shows his love
by licking my face again&again&again.

But I live alone
and because I feel so lonely
as of late,
I dare not let Muggs lie
whether asleep or awake.

# 100% Proof Self-Defense Manual
### *(Homily Grits #8)*

Rule #1, when the fun goes away
in your quarrel with two brothers
(or any others of the same last name)
and blood turns thicker than water:
quick, before you start acting frisky
put in the water a big shot of whiskey.

# Henry's Proof of Free Will
## *(Homily Grits #9)*

Our widowed Aunt Beth had a big pile of money
and an only child (cousin "Hank") named Henry.
She always gave him some good advice,
e.g., "Only fools play games with dice"
because all gamblers end up losers,
or "Beggars can't be choosers"
when young Hank could never find
either a wife or job to suit his mind.
Well, as we read in Aunt Beth's will, much later,
Hank did just fine when he chose to be a beggar.

# Acquiring a Taste for Anthropology
*(Homily Grits #10)*

We studied in our thick textbook
how people from snooty cultures
should give a more complex look
at primitive societies, which have values
we could right away recognize, not despise,
and whose speech, translated, we already know!
Take the Tibi-Tibi from deep inside of Borneo,
a tribe of cannibals, or maybe formerly so,
who gather to chant this familiar dictum:
"Two Heads Are Much Better Than One."
                    (quote, page 147, in *Anthro Intro*)

# What Are Little Girls Made of?
### *(Homily Grits #11)*

Lydia is really a perfect child,
never wild, like some, a darling
and quite bright for a girl of four.
Once Grandma woke her up (awfully soon)
by calling (awfully loud) to her room:
"Don't forget what the early bird catches!"
And kind Lydia, the thoughtful little soul,
politely put it in Grandma's breakfast bowl.

# A Boyfriend's Time Warp
*(Homily Grits #12)*

You complained
you had no uses for excuses.
You pointed at a calendar
with its plainly marked date.
My roses went without water or vase.
Maybe all this made me right last night
when we had our big debate
and I spoke the feeble joke
"Better never than be late."

# Polonius' Portfolio?
### *(Homily Grits #13)*

My father-in-law was quick to point out
he was smarter than most folks hereabout
and true he knew
lots of famous quotes from books
such as Shakespeare's admonition
"Neither a borrower nor a lender be,"
his favorite. Sadly for my wife and me
her daddy died last May (in total penury).

## Mother's Day Poem
*(Homily Grits #14)*

To My Own Mom:
Thanks for helping me along.
You make me work hard on stuff
so I'll grow up tough.
Dad sure is right
when he tells me at night,
"Bless your mother, Willie,
she somehow invented necessity."

# Waiting for the 10<sup>th</sup> Cat
*(Homily Grits #15)*

Of all the promised ways
I ever heard to skin a cat
I quickly found
by far the worst
was not to kill it first.

## Waste Not Why Not
*(Homily Grits #16)*


Vomit thinks the gourmet dog
is free soufflé,
hot rainbow without wet rain:
waste not, want not.

On the other hand
(or in another mouth)
revulsion says it in reverse:
want not, waste not.

Or to consider this whole question
with its gooey sidewalk sight
might be a want you want to waste:
waste want, not not.

# Teacher of the Town
*(Homily Grits #17)*

Edward taught English. For 36 years.
Same little town. Same little school.
Made no money. Earned lots of pride.
Came retirement day. Gave a speech:
"Wasn't very easy. But let me just tell
you again: All's well that ends good."
His old pupils applauded. Even stood.

# Dieting for Health & Safety
*(Homily Grits #18)*

They saved money for a decade
or more, did my wife's folks,
and took their trip to the pyramids,
went along the Nile, all the while
thrilled to be as adventuresome as anyone.
Suddenly—our worst fears!—came the calls,
the tears, even a lawyer with a cruel subpoena.

We found that Egypt has a feisty way
of adopting our very own S.P.C.A.
How to put this without hurting feelings?
Okay, think back to that old tale
of the camel and the final straw,
and in the place of one of those
substitute my mother-in-law.

# How Much Do I Love Thee?
*(Homily Grits #19)*

My dearest Mabel:
At last I'm able to send a letter
and explain better why the delay
to say goodbye to ex-friend Beth.
You see now my mom hit it on the head
when she said those words about how
absence can make the heart grow fonder,
and Mabel, to multiply my love for you,
I'll stay down here a month or two longer.

## How to Make a Poem Shorter Than Its Title
*(Homily Grits #20)*

Here's proof haste
saves space.

www.ingramcontent.com/pod-product-compliance
Lightning Source LLC
Chambersburg PA
CBHW030509130626
46549CB00007B/2899